Jobs in Our Community

Doctors on the Job

By Lorraine Harrison

KidHaven Publishing

Published in 2017 by
KidHaven Publishing, an Imprint of Greenhaven Publishing, LLC
353 3rd Avenue
Suite 255
New York, NY 10010

Designer: Deanna Paternostro
Editor: Katie Kawa

Photo credits: Cover michaeljung/iStock/Thinkstock; pp. 5, 19, 21 Wavebreakmedia Ltd/Thinkstock; p. 7 (top left) Digital Vision/Photodisc/Thinkstock; pp. 7 (bottom left), 9, 11 monkeybusinessimages/iStock/Thinkstock; p. 7 (right) Michael Blann/DigitalVision/Thinkstock; p. 13 George Doyle/Stockbyte/Thinkstock; p. 15 moodboard/Thinkstock; p. 17 didedign021/iStock/Thinkstock; p. 23 BananaStock/Thinkstock; p. 24 (hospital) Pete Spiro/Shutterstock.com.

Library of Congress Cataloging-in-Publication Data

Names: Harrison, Lorraine, author.
Title: Doctors on the job / Lorraine Harrison.
Description: New York : KidHaven Press, [2017] | Series: Jobs in our community | Includes bibliographical references and index.
Identifiers: LCCN 2016036201 (print) | LCCN 2016037408 (ebook) | ISBN 9781534521377 (pbk.) | ISBN 9781534521384 (6 pack) | ISBN 9781534521391 (library bound) | ISBN 9781534521407 (E-book)
Subjects: LCSH: Physicians–Juvenile literature. | Medicine–Juvenile literature.
Classification: LCC R690 .H383 2017 (print) | LCC R690 (ebook) | DDC 610.69/5–dc23
LC record available at https://lccn.loc.gov/2016036201

Printed in the United States of America

CPSIA compliance information: Batch #CW17KL: For further information contact Greenhaven Publishing LLC, New York, New York at 1-844-317-7404.

CONTENTS

Doctors have an important job. They help us stay healthy.

There are many different kinds of doctors. They all work very hard!

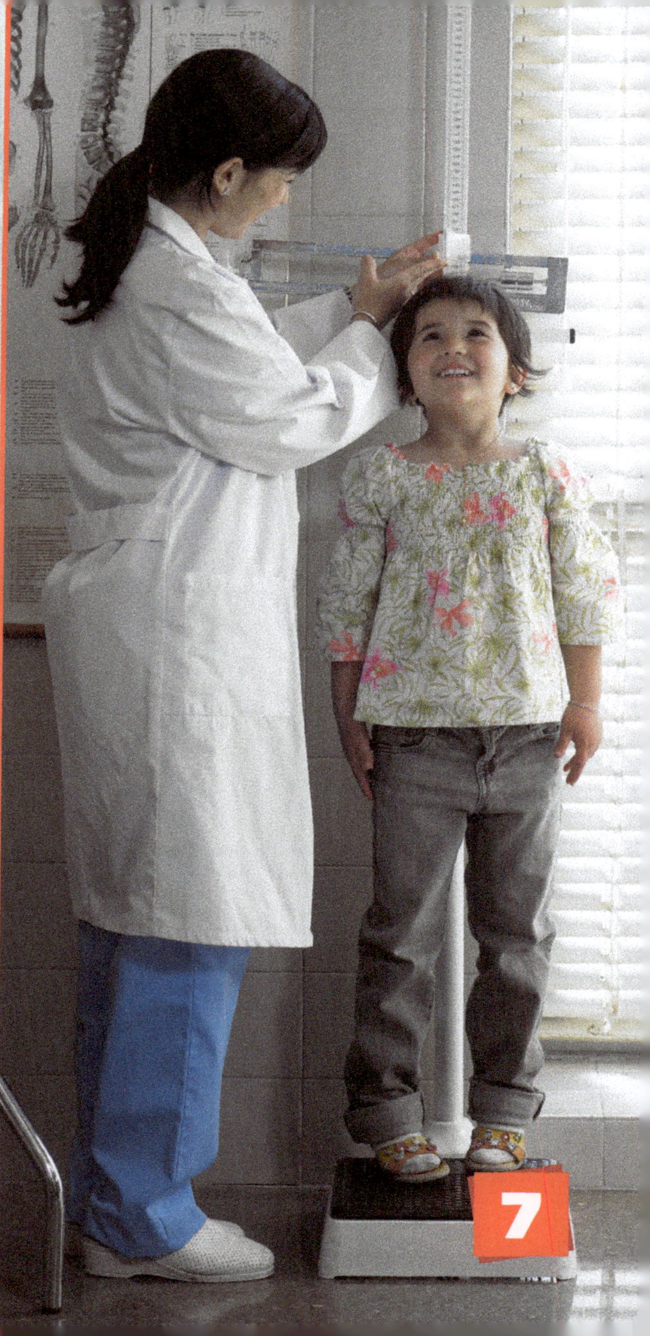

Some doctors work in a **hospital**. People go there when they are very sick or hurt.

Other doctors work in their own office. They have helpers called nurses.

A doctor listens to a person's heart. They use a tool called a **stethoscope**.

Doctors give people **medicine** if they are sick. Medicine can help them feel better.

Doctors also give people shots. Shots help people stay healthy.

Some doctors help people with broken bones. They look at pictures of bones called X-rays.

A doctor puts a **cast** on a person with a broken bone. This helps the bone heal.

Doctors take good care of people in their community!

WORDS TO KNOW

cast

hospital

medicine

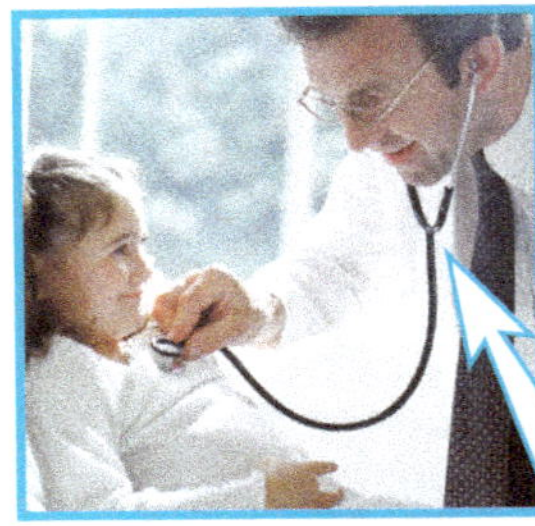

stethoscope

INDEX